4912

'OHANA

LET US MAKE ONE POINT,
THAT WE MEET EACH OTHER WITH
A SMILE, WHEN IT IS DIFFICULT TO SMILE.
SMILE AT EACH OTHER, MAKE TIME FOR
EACH OTHER IN YOUR FAMILY.

—Mother Teresa,
from her Nobel lecture

'OHANA

Mutual Publishing

❋ ❋ ❋

Compiled and designed by Jane Hopkins
Edited by Betty Santos
The quilt pattern designs throughout the book created and © by Poakalani

Backcover: Haili Family, 1920-1921. L.R. Sullivan (Bishop Museum)

First Printing, July 2002
1 2 3 4 5 6 7 8 9

Mutual Publishing
1215 Center Street, Suite 210
Honolulu, Hawai'i 96816
Ph: (808) 732-1709 / Fax: (808) 734-4094
e-mail: mutual@lava.net / www.mutualpublishing.com

Printed in Korea

✺ ✺ ✺

'Ohana refers to the family unit.
I am privileged to be part of an *'ohana*
that is very close knit and connected through a
strong, spiritual foundation. At a very young age,
before going to bed, the *'ohana* would always
gather for family prayers. We actually grew up
understanding that the word *'ohana* usually
referred to "family prayer." It wasn't until later
in life that I learned that *pule* or prayer was
so much a part of family life that the word
'ohana is often used to mean *pule 'ohana*. We re-
cited verses from the Bible, some in English and
some in Hawaiian. The most popular verse was
"Aloha ke Akua...God is Love." We often
chose this verse not only for its simplicity,
but also for its deep, spiritual meaning.
This is a phrase often used by my uncle,
Kahu Abraham Akaka, a well-respected
spiritual leader in Hawai'i.

—Daniel "Kaniela" Akaka Jr.

※ ※ ※

MEMBERS OF THE ʻOHANA, LIKE TARO SHOOTS, ARE ALL FROM THE SAME ROOT.

—Mary Kawena Pukui

The ʻohana is the foundation of Hawaiian culture. The word is loosely translated to mean family, but its significance is much more important. ʻOhana encompasses far more than the Western concept of the nuclear family or even the extended family that would include grandparents, aunts, uncles, and cousins.

The ʻohana can include those born with blood ties, those accepted by marriage, or hānai (adopted), deceased and spiritual ancestors, as well as those tied to the same ʻaina.

Kalo, or taro, was the staff of life for Hawaiians. It was also the source of the origin of the Hawaiian people through the story of Hāloa. Hawaiians consider Hāloa, the first kalo plant, to be their ancestor, who was born first in their world to provide sustenance for all those who would follow.

❋ ❋ ❋

The *kalo* is the only one of the Hawaiian food plants to be propagated by *'oha*, or offshoots, that sprout from the *makua* (the parent), or main corm. This idea reinforces the belief that the continuum between generations is important, that an individual alone is unthinkable.

Each contributes to the welfare of the family. For instance, the *kupuna* provide wisdom and guidance, especially to the *keiki*, the *makua* perform the work that gives daily sustenance, and even the *'aumakua*, or spiritual guardians, provide strength and inspiration. The *'ohana* is the central force that provides for the economic, social and educational needs of all of its members.

The attitudes and ideals of the Hawaiian *'ohana* are echoed in the customs of many ethnic groups that have settled and intermingled with the host culture of Hawai'i.

✳ ✳ ✳

'Ohana is the center of
all things Hawaiian, in this nucleus is
where one learns the values of love, respect,
hospitality, *kōkua,* and forgiveness. This is where all
can learn to be open-minded with one another and
to prepare themselves for the world outside
of the core *'OHANA* where it is *PA'A.*

—Casey Ku'uhoa Ballao

✳ ✳ ✳

KUʻU Ē WE, KUʻU PIKO, KUʻU IWI, KUʻU KOKO.

My umbilical cord, my navel, my bones, my blood.

✻ ✻ ✻

HO'OKĀHI NO HULU LIKE O IA PO'E.

Those people are all of the same feather.

✻ ✻ ✻

O KA MAKUA KE KOʻO O KA HALE E PAʻA AI.

The parent is the support that holds the household together.

✻ ✻ ✻

**TO FORGET ONE'S ANCESTORS
IS TO BE A BROOK WITHOUT A SOURCE,
A TREE WITHOUT A ROOT.**

—Chinese proverb

✳ ✳ ✳

I KA MOA I HĀNAI IĀ I KA LĀ.
I ʻOI AKU MAMUA O KA MOA I HANA
I IĀ I KA MALU.

A rooster fed in the sun is stronger
than one fed in the shade.

(To make him strong, bring your son up in the sun.)

✻ ✻ ✻

**THE GOODNESS OF THE FATHER
REACHES HIGHER THAN A MOUNTAIN;
THAT OF THE MOTHER GOES DEEPER
THAN THE OCEAN.**

—Japanese proverb

✻ ✻ ✻

A FAMILY IS A PLACE
WHERE MINDS COME INTO
CONTACT WITH ONE ANOTHER.
IF THESE MINDS LOVE ONE ANOTHER
THE HOME WILL BE AS BEAUTIFUL AS
A FLOWER GARDEN. BUT IF THESE
MINDS GET OUT OF HARMONY WITH
ONE ANOTHER IT IS LIKE A STORM
THAT PLAYS HAVOC WITH
THE GARDEN.

—Buddha

✻ ✻ ✻

PIPILI NO KA PĪLALI I KE KUMU KUKUI.

The pīlai gum sticks to the kukui tree.

**(Said of one who remains close to a
loved one all the time, as a child may
cling to the grandparent he loves.)**

✻ ✻ ✻

**TELL ME WHO YOUR FATHER IS,
AND I'LL TELL YOU WHO YOU ARE.**

—Filipino proverb

✳ ✳ ✳

LUHI WAHINE ʻIA.

Labored over by a woman.

**(Spoken in respect and admiration of a
family reared by a woman who alone
fed and clothed them.)**

✳ ✳ ✳

**BROTHERS AND SISTERS ARE
AS CLOSE AS HANDS AND FEET.**

—Vietnamese proverb

❀ ❀ ❀

GOVERN A FAMILY AS YOU WOULD COOK A SMALL FISH—VERY GENTLY.

—Chinese proverb

HE MEA LOA'A 'OLE KA HULU MAKUA.

You will never find another parent.

✽ ✽ ✽

UA PŌMAIKA'I KĀUA, OLA NĀ IWI I LOKO O KŌ KAUA MAU LĀ 'ELEMAKULE.

We two are indeed fortunate, we shall be cared for in the days of our old age.

✺ ✺ ✺

WHEN YOU HAVE CHILDREN YOURSELF, YOU BEGIN TO UNDERSTAND WHAT YOU OWE YOUR PARENTS.

—Japanese proverb

NO KEKAHI O KĀKOU KA PILIKIA, MALAILA PU KĀKOU A PAU.

Should one of us get into trouble,
we will all go that way.

(Adversity to one is adversity to all.)

✻ ✻ ✻

THE HOUSE WITH AN OLD GRANDPARENT HARBORS A JEWEL.

—Chinese proverb

✻ ✻ ✻

**CHILDREN YOKE PARENTS TO
THE PAST, PRESENT, AND FUTURE.**

—Japanese proverb

✻ ✻ ✻

NAU KE KEIKI, KŪKAE A NAʻAU.

Yours is the child, excreta, intestines and all.

(In giving a child to adoptive parents, the true parents warned that under no condition would they take the child back. To do so would be disastrous for the child. Recognition, love, and help might continue; but removal while the adoptive parents live—never.)

✺ ✺ ✺

**IF THE MAIN TIMBERS IN
THE HOUSE ARE NOT STRAIGHT,
THE SMALLER TIMBER WILL BE UNSAFE;
AND IF THE SMALLER TIMBERS ARE NOT
STRAIGHT, THE HOUSE WILL FALL.**

—Chinese proverb

※ ※ ※

I KA NOHO PU ANA ʻIKE I KE ALOHA.

One sees love after living together.

✳ ✳ ✳

IN DWELLING,
LIVE CLOSE TO THE GROUND.

IN THINKING, KEEP TO THE SIMPLE.

IN CONFLICT, BE FAIR AND GENEROUS.

IN GOVERNING,
DON'T TRY TO CONTROL.

IN WORK, DO WHAT YOU ENJOY.

IN FAMILY LIFE, BE COMPLETELY PRESENT.

—Tao Te Ching

❋ ❋ ❋

KA HANA A KA MĀKUA,
O KA HANA NO IA A KEIKI.

What parents do, children will do.

❋ ❋ ❋

ʻA ʻOHE IPU ʻŌPIO E ʻOLE KA MIMINO I KA LĀ.

No immature gourd can withstand
withering in the sun (without care).

(No child can get along without adult supervision.)

LISTEN TO THE WISDOM
OF THE TOOTHLESS ONES.

—Fijian proverb

✳ ✳ ✳

MAI KĀPAE I KE AʻO A KA MAKUA, AIA HE OLA MALAILA.

Do not set aside the teachings of one's
parents for there is life there.

I MAIKAʻI KE KALO I KA ʻOHĀ.

The goodness of the taro is judged
by the young plant it produces.

(Parents are often judged by the behavior of their children.)

✳ ✳ ✳

UA ʻAI AU I KANA LOAʻA.

I have eaten of his gain.

**(Said with pride and affection by a parent
or grandparent who is being cared
for by the child he reared.)**

✻ ✻ ✻

WITH ALL BEINGS AND ALL THINGS
WE SHALL BE AS RELATIVES.

—Sioux Indian

NA WAI HOʻI KA ʻOLE O KE AKAMAI, HE ALANUI I MAʻA I KA HELE ʻIA E OʻU MAU MĀKUA?

Why shouldn't I know, when it is a
road often traveled by my parents?

(Reply of King Liholiho when someone praised his wisdom.)

❇ ❇ ❇

EVEN CHILDREN OF THE SAME MOTHER LOOK DIFFERENT.

—Korean proverb

✻ ✻ ✻

ʻIKE AKU, ʻIKE MAI, KŌKUA AKU KŌKUA MAI; PELA IHO LA KA NOHONA ʻOHANA.

Recognize and be recognized, help and be helped; such is family life.

✳ ✳ ✳

**CRABS TEACH THEIR OFFSPRING
TO WALK STRAIGHT.**

—Malaysian proverb

�֎ ✖ ✖

BIBLIOGRAPHY

Judd, Henry P. *Hawaiian Proverbs and Riddles.* Honolulu: Bernice P. Bishop Museum, Bulletin 77, 1930.

Pukui, Mary Kawena. *'Olelo No'eau: Hawaiian Proverbs and Poetical Sayings.* Honolulu: Bishop Museum Special Publication No. 71, 1983.

de Ley, Gerd. *International Dictionary of Proverbs.* New York: Hippocrene Books, 1998.

Galef, David, ed. *Even Monkeys Fall From Trees.* Boston: Tuttle Publishing, 1987.

Steichen, Edward. *The Family of Man.* New York: The Museum of Modern Art, 1955.

The Quotations Page, http://tqpage.com. *Laura Moncur's Motivational Quotations.* 1994

_____. *Cole's Quotables.* 1994

✳ ✳ ✳

PHOTO CREDITS

Page 2: Charles K. Kamahoahoa Family, 1920-21. L.R. Sullivan (Bishop Museum)

Page 5: The Toomey Family, 1916. (Baker-Van Dyke)

Page 6: Noa Kaopuiki and others, 1921. K.P. Emory (Bishop Museum)

Page 11: Mrs. James Kahoilihala, 1920-21. Sullivan Collection (Bishop Museum)

Page 13: Mrs. John Haili and daughter, Dorothy. 1920-21, L.R. Sullivan (Bishop Museum)

Page 15: Kamakahi Family, 1920-21. L.R. Sullivan (Bishop Muscum)

Page 17: Antone Gasper Family, 1920-21. L.R. Sullivan (Bishop Museum)

Page 19: See Young Yap and family, 1900. (Kathleen T. O. Chang Collection)

Page 21: John Haili and son, John Haili, Jr. 1920-21. L.R. Sullivan (Bishop Museum)

Page 22: Japanese family in front of car with a house in the background. Usaku Teragawachi (Bishop Museum)

Page 24: Chinese wedding party, ca. 1930. On Char (Bishop Museum)

Page 27: Mr. Daniel Ho'olapa with wife and grandchildren, 1925. Theodore Kelsey (June Gutmanis Collection)

Page 29: Filipino family, ca . 1920. On Char (Bishop Museum)

Page 30: Mrs. Kalaau and young boys, 1920-21. L. R. Sullivan (Bishop Museum)

Page 33: Hawaiian children, 1897-1901. Davey (Bishop Museum)

Page 35: Chinese family in front of their plantation house. (Lyman House Memorial Museum)

Page 37: Hawaiian girl in her father's arms. (Bishop Museum)

Page 39: Kauhane Apiki and wife, Hoohuli Apiki,1921. K. P. Emory (Bishop Museum)

Page 41: Two women with three children wearing paper leis. Usaku Teragawachi (Bishop Museum)

Page 43: Group photo, c. 1900. (Bishop Museum)

Page 45: Mrs. Wilmot Vrendenburg and grandson, Wilmot, 1920-21. Sullivan Collection (Bishop Museum)

Page 47: Japanese family, ca. 1930. (Alexander & Baldwin Sugar Museum)

Page 49: Mr. and Mrs. David Kawai and niece Annabel, 1921. K. P. Emory (Bishop Museum)

Page 51: Chinese family members, c. 1935. On Char (Bishop Museum)

Page 52: Mr. and Mrs. Kauhane Kukololoua, 1921. K. P. Emory (Bishop Museum)

Page 54: Portuguese family. (Hawai'i State Archives)

Page 56: John Maliko Kekua and children, 1920-21. L. R. Sullivan (Bishop Museum)

Page 58: Unidentified. (Hawai'i State Archives)

Page 60: S.W. Kiuo, 1920-21. L. R. Sullivan (Bishop Museum)

Page 62: Matthaias H. Akona and family, 1920-21. L. R. Sullivan (Bishop Museum)

Page 65: Hawaiian family among the taro. (Baker-Van Dyke)

Page 67: Mother and daughter, c. 1890. (Hawai'i State Archives)

Page 68: Mrs. Luhiau and family, 1920-21. Sullivan Collection (Bishop Museum)

Page 70: Keong Lee and wife Ualani Kaia and children, 1915-1920. On Char (Bishop Museum)

Page 72: Korean family, 1915-1920. On Char (Bishop Museum)

Page 75: Keanu Family at Kahea, Lana'i, 1921. K. P. Emory (Bishop Museum)

Page 77: Daguerreotype of the Lyman family about 1853. (Baker-Van Dyke)